EXPLORING WORLD CULTURES

Dominican Republic

Laura L. Sullivan

Cavendish
Square
New York

Published in 2017 by Cavendish Square Publishing, LLC
243 5th Avenue, Suite 136, New York, NY 10016

Library of Congress Cataloging-in-Publication Data

Names: Sullivan, Laura L., 1974-
Title: Dominican Republic / Laura L. Sullivan.
Description: New York : Cavendish Square Publishing, 2017. | Series: Exploring world cultures | Includes bibliographical
references and index. | Description based on print version record and CIP data provided by publisher; resource not viewed.
Identifiers: LCCN 2015051329 (print) | LCCN 2015050686 (ebook) | ISBN 9781502617354 (ebook) | ISBN 9781502618061
(paperback) | ISBN 9781502617989 (library bound) | ISBN 9781502617811 (6 pack)
Subjects: LCSH: Dominican Republic--Juvenile literature.
Classification: LCC F1934.2 (print) | LCC F1934.2 .S85 2017 (ebook) | DDC 972.93--dc23
LC record available at http://lccn.loc.gov/2015051329

Editorial Director: David McNamara
Editor: Kristen Susienka
Copy Editor: Rebecca Rohan
Art Director: Jeffrey Talbot
Designer: Joseph Macri
Production Assistant: Karol Szymczuk
Photo Research: J8 Media

Printed in the United States of America

Contents

Introduction

The Dominican Republic is part of an island in the Caribbean Sea. It shares the island with another country, Haiti. Many tourists visit the Dominican Republic each year. Though it is best known for its clean, beautiful beaches, the Dominican Republic has mountains and rain forests, too. Tourists can stay in resorts and enjoy year-round golfing.

The Dominican Republic has its own **culture**. It has many styles of dancing, music, and art. At night, **merengue** music can be heard almost everywhere. Visitors are welcomed.

The Dominican Republic is a **diverse** country. Many people from the Dominican Republic have ancestors from other countries.

4

People have lived in the Dominican Republic for about two thousand years. The nation has had problems and good times. Parts of the country are very poor. Other parts are trying to become more modern. The Dominican Republic is a country that remembers its history and tries to create a better place to live.

The Dominican Republic attracts millions of tourists each year.

This map shows the states that make up the Dominican Republic. The country of Haiti is on the left-hand side.

The Dominican Republic is on the island of Hispaniola. It takes up about two-thirds of the island, on the east side. It has an area of about 18,704 square miles (48,442 square kilometers). On the west side of the island is its neighbor, Haiti.

The country has four main mountain ranges, four major rivers, and wide valleys. It is best known

A rhinoceros iguana

for its beaches along the coast of the beautiful Caribbean Sea.

Because of its mountains, the country sees many kinds of weather. The coast is hot and wet. A hurricane strikes every few years. The mountains are much cooler. Sometimes it even snows in the mountains.

High and Low Places

The Dominican Republic has both the highest and lowest points in the Caribbean. The highest point is Pico Duarte at 10,164 feet (3,098 meters) above sea level. The lowest point is the salt lake Enriquillo, at 148 feet (45 m) below sea level.

People called the **Taíno** lived alone on the island from 650 CE until Christopher Columbus landed on Hispaniola in 1492. At first, the Spanish and Taíno got along. Later,

This image shows a Taíno person cooking fish.

they fought. Many Taíno died from diseases like smallpox.

Afterward, the island was ruled by Spain, then by France. In 1821, the Dominican Republic became independent. In 1822, Haiti took over. Eventually, the Dominican Republic regained its independence in 1844.

Rock Art

The Pomier Caves show rock art from as far back as two thousand years ago. The Taíno created some of the artwork.

Cave paintings show the country's history and wildlife.

Cruel leaders called dictators ran the country in the twentieth century. Some dictators helped the country become better, but they also hurt people. By the 1980s, the country was improving. Eventually, the dictators lost power. Today, the Dominican Republic is a **democracy**.

FACT!

Rafael Trujillo was a cruel dictator. Though he improved the country's economy, he tortured or murdered anyone who was against him.

VOTE ✓

Citizens of the Dominican Republic elect people to represent them. Elections choose presidents, vice presidents, and senators.

President Danilo Medina

The country has three branches of government: executive, legislative, and judicial. The executive branch is headed by the president. There is a vote for president and vice president every four years. The president

FACT!

The capital of the Dominican Republic is officially called Santo Domingo de Guzmán, but most people call it Santo Domingo.

selects members to help him. The president is also the head of the military. The legislative branch includes a 32-member senate and the Chamber of Deputies, which has

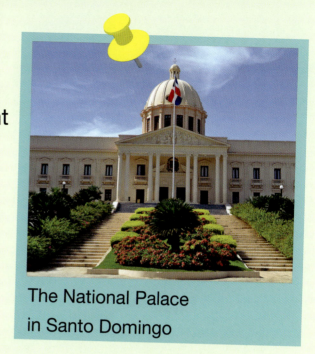

The National Palace in Santo Domingo

178 members. The legislative branch makes the laws. The judicial branch interprets the laws and makes sure people follow them.

Many Constitutions

Since it became independent in 1844, the Dominican Republic has had thirty-eight different **constitutions.** That is more than any other country.

Many tourists enjoy whale watching in the Dominican Republic.

Today, the Dominican Republic has a good economy. Mining and farming bring money to the country. The largest industry is tourism. Visitors who stay in hotels, eat at restaurants, and shop add lots of money to the economy.

However, there are some problems. Electricity is found in most areas, but sometimes it does not

The national currency is called the peso. In 2015, one US dollar was worth 45 pesos.

The Dominican peso

work. On farms, some young children work. This is not good since children need to go to school. There are many poor people in the country, too. Not everyone is treated the same in the Dominican Republic. If people have money, they can live well there. If they do not have money, they face problems.

Ecotourism

Ecotourism helps the country's economy grow. People visit natural places to see wildlife in their own habitat and help protect the animals' homes.

The environment is important to the Dominican Republic. It is not always easy to take care of it, though.

Birds and mammals live on land and in the sea. In the Caribbean,

Humpback whales give birth near the Dominican Republic.

coral reefs are home to hundreds of kinds of fish. Every year, humpback whales gather near the island to give birth. American crocodiles mostly live in salt water but can go in fresh water, too.

FACT!

The Dominican Republic has 5,600 kinds of plants and 303 kinds of birds.

On the border between Haiti and the Dominican Republic, there is a lot of pollution and destruction of forests. Harsh weather and humans break down the soil. Humans cut down trees. This hurts the environment. Pollution from Haiti also affects the Dominican Republic.

Beware the Shrew

The *Hispaniolan solenodon* is an endangered animal that looks like a large shrew. It is one of the few venomous mammals. Deadly spit runs through a groove in its tooth.

Watch out for his bite!

The population of the Dominican Republic mostly comes from mixed Spanish, African, and Taíno backgrounds.

About ten million people live in the Dominican Republic. The majority are mixed race. That means they have ancestors who came from both Europe and Africa. About 16 percent of the population is white and 11 percent is black.

Many people from the Dominican Republic are also part Native American. Even though there

aren't any members of the Taíno tribe left, part of their **DNA** remains in the population.

There are many immigrants in the country. They mostly come from other Caribbean nations. Others come from places like China, Japan, and Spain.

Most of the population lives in cities. Nearly three million people live in Santo Domingo. About 31 percent of the population is under age fifteen. Only 6 percent is over age sixty-five.

Discovering Ancestors

Scientists can study DNA to find out where a person's ancestors came from.

The family is the most important connection in Dominican life.

In the Dominican Republic, family is very important. Three or more generations often live in the same neighborhood. Sometimes they even live in the same house. Family members are loyal to each other and treat each other with respect.

FACT!

The Dominican Republic lifestyle is a mix of European, African, and Taíno traditions.

Dominicans are known for their hospitality. Guests are welcomed with enthusiasm. People go out of their way to make guests feel welcome.

By law, Dominican women are equal to men in all ways. However, that is not always true in life. Women are sometimes expected to stay at home and take care of their families instead of working. In many families, the oldest male makes the important decisions.

Women in Elections

A law states that at least 33 percent of candidates for all elections must be female.

Religion

There are many religions in the Dominican Republic. Anyone living there can practice any religion, or no religion at all. The majority of people—about 69 percent—are Roman

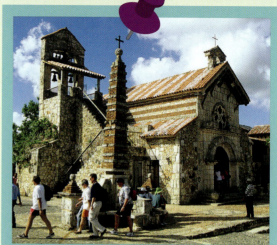

A Catholic church in the Dominican Republic

Catholic. About 18 percent are Protestant. A little over 10 percent have no religion. Other religions include Buddhism, Islam, and Judaism.

Many Religions

Several Afro-Caribbean religions are practiced here, including Dominican Vodou and Congos del Espiritu Santo.

Some religious people go to church every week. Even those who don't go all the time often go to the church for special occasions like weddings, baptisms, or certain holidays.

Some Christian religions include aspects of African religions and cultures. Africans were originally brought to the country as slaves. Some of their beliefs and traditions have been adopted by the people of the Dominican Republic.

FACT!

During World War II, Jews escaping from Europe went to live in the Dominican Republic. They founded the city of Sosua.

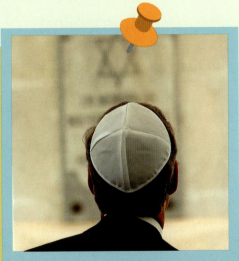

The city of Sosua has a large Jewish population.

Language

Spanish is the main language spoken in the Dominican Republic. Nearly everyone speaks it. It has different sounds and words than the type of Spanish spoken in Spain. It is called Dominican Spanish.

Students learn to speak other languages in school.

Dominican Spanish is unique to the country. It is a mix of old Taíno words and Spanish words.

Common Words

English speakers use some Taíno words, such as barbecue, hammock, canoe, hurricane, and iguana.

Many Chinese immigrants arrived in the Dominican Republic in the 1800s and 1900s. Today, Chinese is becoming a more popular language there.

Some of the Spanish words are so old they are no longer spoken in Spain.

At school, children are taught in Spanish. Most children also learn English and French.

Another language spoken in the country is Haitian Creole. It is spoken by Haitians living in the Dominican Republic. About eight thousand people speak Samaná English. This form of English was first spoken by black people who moved to the Dominican Republic in the 1820s.

These performers walk in a parade to celebrate Carnival.

Many people play merengue music in the Dominican Republic. It is fast music played with drums, trumpets, saxophones, and the accordion. Another form of music is bachata. It is both a type of music and a type of dance. Dominican rock is also popular.

The Dominican Republic has many festivals. The biggest are the carnivals held in February.

Music, dancing, and parades are common. There are also festivals during the week before Easter. In June, a festival celebrates African music.

The country has produced many artists. A popular style of art is folk art. It is painted with many bright colors. Folk art can be masks, paintings, or statues. It is popular with tourists who visit the country.

A Food Festival

Taste Santo Domingo is a big October food festival. Restaurants share their food with thousands of people, and chefs compete in contests.

Fun and Play

Most Dominicans enjoy the warm weather by spending a lot of time outside. Just like the tourists who visit, residents often go to the beach or enjoy scuba diving or snorkeling. Fishing, surfing, or boating are also popular with many Dominicans.

Both tourists and Dominicans enjoy scuba diving and snorkeling.

Winning in the Olympics

Several Dominicans have won Olympic medals in track and field events, tae kwon do, and boxing. Athlete Felix Sanchez won a gold medal in hurdles for the country in 2012.

Baseball is the most popular sport in the Dominican Republic. Children often learn to play at a young age. Adults support the country's baseball league, which has six teams.

Pedro Martinez is one of many baseball players from the Dominican Republic to join Major League Baseball.

Other sports in the country include basketball, soccer, and volleyball. Boxing is also extremely popular. Many world champion boxers come from the Dominican Republic.

FACT!

Dominoes is a game many Dominicans enjoy. Both children and adults play the game.

Food

There are many types of food in the Dominican Republic. Lots of food comes from Spanish culture, Africa, and from meals the Taíno made.

A meal called *la bandera*

Most meals include some kind of meat. Pork is a favorite throughout the country, and seafood is eaten near the coast. Breakfast might be mashed plantains, fried eggs, fried salami, fried

FACT!

Many dishes in the Dominican Republic use sofrito, a blend of herbs and spices including garlic, onion, peppers, paprika, cilantro, and oregano. It is cooked in olive oil or animal fat.

cheese, and avocado. Lunch is usually the biggest meal of the day. Rice, beans, and some kind of meat are often served. Dinner is usually lighter.

A meal called *los tres golpes*

An Old Meal

Guanimos are a kind of food that can be traced back to the Taíno people. Cornmeal is stuffed with meat or another filling, wrapped in banana leaf or cornhusks, and cooked.

Glossary

constitution A document that describes the laws of a country.

culture A word describing a country's identity by its music, customs, and languages.

democracy A kind of government where citizens vote for people to represent them.

diverse Having a lot of variety.

DNA The part of a cell in the body that carries genetic information.

ecotourism Visiting a place to learn about its environment and nature.

merengue A fast style of music that began in the Dominican Republic.

Taíno An ancient group of people that lived in the Caribbean, especially the Dominican Republic.

Find Out More

Books

Alvarez, Julia. *How Tia Lola Came to (Visit) Stay*.
New York: Random House, 2001.

Tavares, Matt. *Growing Up Pedro*. Somerville, MA:
Candlewick Press, 2015.

Website

Embassy of the Dominican Republic: Kids' Corner

www.domrep.org/kids.html

Video

Travel Channel: Dominican Republic

www.travelchannel.com/destinations/dominican-republic/santo-domingo/video/best-of-the-dominican-republic

Watch this short video about the beauty of the Dominican Republic.

Index

About the Author

Laura L. Sullivan has written more than thirty fiction and nonfiction books for children, including many for Cavendish Square Publishing. *Life As a Spy in the American Revolution*, *Life as an Explorer with Lewis and Clark*, and *Life as a Passenger on the Mayflower* are among her favorites.